All About Your Goldfish

Contents

Goldfish
are simple and inexpensive to keep, and can make an excellent introduction to the world of fishkeeping. But even though goldfish can be considered the ultimate low-maintenance pet, they still have their own specific needs, and must be properly cared for throughout their lives.

Of course, fish are pretty different to mammals, which include most of our household pets as well as ourselves.

● Fish are cold-blooded, which means that their body temperature depends upon the temperature of the environment around them. If this temperature drops, their body metabolism will slow down.

● As fish live in water they do not have lungs. They breathe with the aid of gills, which are very sensitive to the quality of the water that surrounds them.

● Their body is covered by a layer of bony scales that overlap each other from the head towards the tail to allow maximum streamlining in the water, aided by a protective layer of mucus on top – which is what makes them as slippery as an eel!

Goldfish – and not-so-gold fish

The good old-fashioned goldfish is an attractive and sturdy fish, with a colour that can vary from a strong golden red to a paler yellow-gold. Others may have patches of silver or black on their body. They are the ideal fish for a beginner, and can be kept in a reasonably-sized indoor tank until they reach about five inches in length, at which point they will need to be transferred to a pond. However, goldfish kept indoors do seem to adapt to the size of tank available, and often remain small enough to be able to continue to live in their original home throughout their lives.

A wide range of different varieties of goldfish have been bred from the basic specimen, and although they are all actually the same species of animal, they vary enormously in colour and body shape.

Goldfish are the ultimate low-maintenance pet but they should still be cared for properly .

Comet

Red and white Comet.

As the name suggests, the Comet is a streamlined version of the goldfish, with an exceptionally long tail-fin that can be as long as its body. This enables it to swim very quickly, so it needs a large tank. They are most commonly plain yellow, but are now widely available with a white body and bright red coloration along their back.

DID YOU KNOW?

Fumes can harm fish, and you should take care if using paint, strong polish or disinfectant near the tank. Insecticide sprays can be particularly harmful, so read the instructions on the can first before using them in the same room.

Shubunkins

These are a distinctively coloured variety of the goldfish, with a striking bluish-silver body mottled with black, red, brown, yellow or violet and a red snout. Bristol Shubunkins have a very long tail-fin and metallic scales, whereas the London Shubunkin has non-metallic scales and fins more like a normal goldfish.

Comet: A streamlined version of the goldfish.

The Bristol Shubunkin has distinctive colouring and a long tail fin.

Twin-Tailed Varieties

These varieties have been bred with double tail and anal fins, and their bodies have been shortened to the point where their swimming is impaired.

They are much less hardy than the common goldfish, and are not suitable for outdoor ponds. They are also much less tolerant of poor water conditions, so are not ideal for beginners.

The Calico Fantail has a short, round body and flowing fins.

Fantail

This is perhaps the most normal of the twin-tailed varieties, and although it has a short, round body and flowing fins, it is generally able to swim normally. If you want something a bit more fancy than a single-tailed goldfish, this is the one for you.

Veiltail

This is similar to the fantail, but the tail-fin hangs in folds and the dorsal (back) fin is very tall. The extreme length of their fins can make swimming difficult, and they can easily damage themselves on any sharp projections around the tank.

Moor

This variety is similar in outline to the veiltail, although the body is even more egg-shaped and the eyes are often 'telescopic' – on the end of stalks sticking out from the head. Their body colour is always jet-black.

The Moor is always jet-black in colour.

Lionhead

This has a short, egg-shaped body and a raspberry-like growth on its head around the eyes. It does not have a dorsal fin, and so is a very ungainly swimmer.

An immature Lionhead: This variety does not have a dorsal fin.

Oranda

This has a similar head development but does have a dorsal fin. The Red-capped Oranda has a white body and a red 'cap' over its head. Weird !

Fancy Fish

There is almost no end to the strange varieties of goldfish that have been bred, such as the Celestial, with eyes that point upwards, and the Pearlscale, with deformed dome-shaped scales, each with a white centre. Frankly, many of these are pretty grotesque, and the healthy agility of a more natural fish is much more desirable to most people. If these fancy varieties are kept, they need excellent water conditions and must be protected from more aggressive fish that may damage them.

The Red - Capped Oranda is similar in head shape to the Lionhead, but it does have a dorsal fin.

The Aquarium

You should have your aquarium up and running before you purchase your fish. Rule number one is not to buy a goldfish bowl. This is because they only allow a very small surface area for oxygen to diffuse into the water, unless they are only half-filled. However, in this case, once some gravel is added to the bottom, it allows very little depth for the fish to swim.

The Tank

A rectangular tank is the best bet, and the all-glass variety is advisable as it is strong and relatively cheap. Plastic tanks are acceptable, but the plastic will tend to scratch with time and lose its clarity. Avoid the old-fashioned type of glass tank with an angle iron frame, as they are much more likely to leak or to go rusty. Some very unusual ornamental tanks are now available, but ensure they are practicable as well as nice to look at.

Buy the largest tank that you can afford, and

that will fit into the available space. A tank 2ft long, 1ft wide and 1ft deep (60cm x 30cm x 30cm) is fine, but if you can stretch to one 3ft long, 15ins wide and 15ins deep (90cm x 40cm x 40cm), so much the better.

The simplest way of keeping a goldfish is in a tank with a cover to prevent any escape attempts, with some aquarium gravel in the bottom of the tank, and some ornaments or plants. Backing sheets, printed with underwater scenes, can be stuck to the back of the tank to hide whatever is behind. These will add interest, and help to shade the tank from direct sunlight.

This basic set-up is perfectly satisfactory providing partial water changes are made regularly.

Special effects

If you want to set up a more ambitious aquarium that will hold more fish and look more attractive, you can add the following:

LIGHTING: Fluorescent lighting is best, as this will not heat up the water as much as ordinary light-bulbs and will last much longer. Special tubes are available to encourage plant growth and show off the fish to their best advantage. A cover glass should be placed on top of the tank to reduce water loss from evaporation, and to shield the lamp-fittings from condensation and splashes.

A box filter can be suspended inside or outside the tank.

FILTRATION: A pump can be used to bubble air through an airstone to help aerate the water, or it can be used to power a filter to help keep the water clean. There are two main types of filter used in freshwater tanks:

Box filter. This can either be inside or suspended outside the tank. It mechanically filters the water that passes through it with filter wool, and can also contain activated charcoal, which will absorb poisons that build up in the water. It does need regular cleaning to keep it functioning properly.

Undergravel filter. This consists of a plate under the gravel that draws the water through it. Natural bacteria in the gravel act as a biological filter and break down the waste products that build up in the water.

An undergravel filter makes use of natural bacteria in the gravel.

Safety first

Water and electricity do not mix well, so follow these rules if you do use electrical equipment such as pumps and lighting with your tank.

● *Ensure they are installed by a QUALIFIED electrician, or someone who is experienced in fitting electrical appliances.*
● *Fit the power supply with a CIRCUIT BREAKER to cut off the power if a leakage of current occurs.*
● *SWITCH OFF the power before handling electrical equipment.*
● *NEVER use switches or touch electrical equipment with wet hands.*

Do not position the tank close to a window, as it will get too hot in summer and the excessive light will encourage green algae to grow in abundance. If you are

going to use artificial lighting and filtration, you will need to have convenient access to a power supply. Once the tank is full of gravel and water it will weigh a considerable amount, so ensure that it is on a sturdy base, and that the floorboards underneath are capable of supporting it.

GRAVEL. If you are using an undergravel filter, this needs to be placed in the tank first and covered with gravel. Use reasonably coarse aquarium gravel; brightly-coloured gravel is available for use in coldwater tanks, but some people prefer the more natural look. It must be washed thoroughly first in running tap-water until the water that runs off is clear. Put an average of two inches into the bottom of the tank, with a gentle gradient from the back of the tank to the front.

ROCKS AND ORNAMENTS. Next you can put rocks and ornaments into the tank, with an appropriate backing sheet for the tank to match the style of what you are going to put inside. Some people like to try and create a natural-looking environment for their fish, others really let their imagination run riot! All manner of decorative items are available for goldfish tanks, such as divers that can be attached to an air-line and emit a stream of bubbles and fantasy castles to create a magical kingdom. Of course, this is for the benefit of the owners and not the fish, but if it's what appeals to you, then why not?

If you are going for the natural look, you will want to put in some rocks, which you may be able to find locally, or can purchase specially for the purpose. Smaller stones can be glued together with silicone adhesive to keep them in place, although this must be allowed to cure in accordance with the directions on the pack before water is added. Use hard stones such as slate or shale, and wash them thoroughly before use.

Setting Up The Tank

ELECTRICAL GEAR Now it's time for the electrical gear, if you are going to use it. An air-pump can be used to power a small internal or external filter, and the air-line can be split so that some of the air output goes through an airstone to aerate the tank.

Ensure that the pump is positioned above the level of the tank, or that it has a non-return valve in the air-line to prevent water siphoning back into the pump when it is switched off. A cover glass can be laid on top of the tank, with a bead of silicone glue under each corner to allow some space for air to circulate from the outside into the tank. The hood and lighting can then be placed on top of this.

THE WATER Finally its time to "fill 'em up". Ordinary tapwater is fine for this job, provided you let it stand for a day to allow the chlorine that is added to the water to clear. Alternatively, you can add a proprietary dechlorinating water treatment that is designed for use with fish. Running the water straight on to the gravel will disturb all your careful tank arrangements. The best method is to gently pour the water into a cup, standing on a saucer, standing on the gravel. The water then spills out of the cup, on to the saucer, and gently into the tank.

Planting Your Tank

Plastic plants are often used by beginners in their tanks, and have some advantages. A newly set up tank has little in the way of natural nutrients in the water, so many pond plants will not survive for long. Even those that do thrive may become stringy and unattractive with time. If algae grows on the plastic plants it can simply be scrubbed off.

However, living plants do have many advantages. They do look more realistic, although some of the better-quality artificial plants are pretty convincing. Growing plants will help to oxygenate the water and remove unwanted waste products that build up, and, if given the right conditions, a small number of plants will multiply to fill the tank. Fish also seem to enjoy plants, and nibble at the leaves.

Pot plants

Many plants are now available grown in small pots filled with rock wool. This is greyish substance that can be impregnated with slow release fertiliser to encourage the plant to grow. This is much better than buying unrooted plants, which very often die before they are able to grow roots in the new tank. Many aquatic plants are able to absorb nutrients from the water through their leaves, and will benefit from the addition of plant conditioning solutions that are designed to be added to fish tanks.

Artificial plants.

Selecting Plants

Be careful to select plants suitable for cold-water aquariums from the wide range that are available. Recommended species include:

Anacharis (formerly Elodea) densa

Commonly known as Canadian pondweed, it bears dark green leaves on long stems that can be cut to the depth of the tank as they grow. It absorbs most of the nutrients it needs through the leaves and tolerates the relatively cool temperatures of a goldfish tank.

Anacharis densa.

Myriophyllum

Commonly known as the water milfoil, it is one of the hardiest aquarium plants suitable for a goldfish aquarium. It develops long, winding stems with many branches that bear long, thin leaves in bushes. Goldfish love the sense of security that the dense cover affords, and it also provides a favourite spawning site. There is even a chance that some fry will escape being eaten if they are born in a community tank thickly planted with this plant. It can be propagated by taking cuttings from the end of long stems, stripping the lower three pairs of leaves and replanting in bunches of four or five stalks.

Myriophyllum.

Microsorium

Easier to remember as Java fern, this is an easy plant to grow in a coldwater aquarium, and has broad leaves that make a very good decoration at the front of the tank. It

Hygrophilia diformis (Water Wisteria)

grows from a rhizome, which is a thickened root that grows over whatever surface it has been planted on, sending out leaves as it goes. Therefore, it should not be planted in the gravel, but attached to the rockwork with rubber bands.

Ludwigia palustris

This plant with rounded leaves is commonly available. Ludwigia polysperma is a similar plant with reddish-coloured leaves – it is slightly more difficult to grow.

When you go to a pet store that specialises in fish, you will see many species of aquatic plants. Many are suitable for a cold-water goldfish aquarium but check that the plants you buy will thrive if they are fully submerged. Marsh-type plants prefer to be semi-submerged, and will rot if they are planted in a goldfish tank.

Ludwigia palustris.

Buying Goldfish

DID YOU KNOW?

The first major public aquarium was opened in the Zoological Gardens of London in 1853.

Go to a reputable pet shop that specialises in fish, where you should be confident of getting healthy livestock and excellent advice. Look for a store that is clean and well-kept, where the

Signs of A Healthy Goldfish

Movement: swimming effortlessly, though long-finned varieties will swim more slowly.

Scales: no sore areas or wooly fungal growths.

Colour: dense and even.

Fins: erect and undamaged.

tanks are well-maintained, and there are no signs of sick or dead fish in any of the tanks. The fish should not be overcrowded in their tanks, and the water should not be cloudy.

Body: well rounded – not excessively thin, but not too distended either.

Eyes: bright and clear.

Gills: rapid movement of the gills can be a sign of ill health, as is gulping at the surface of the water.

Buying A Goldfish

How many?

We don't know if goldfish get lonely, but their relatives live in groups in the wild, so it is reasonable to assume they are most comfortable that way. It is certainly more interesting to keep a few smaller goldfish in a tank rather than just one big one, but bullying can occur, so observe them closely, particularly if you notice torn fins. The slower and less hardy twin-tailed goldfish are best kept with their own kind, and goldfish should not be mixed with wild-caught native fish as this can introduce disease and they are unlikely to settle down together.

The number of fish that can be kept in an aquarium will depend on a number of factors, such as:

● The size of the tank, especially the surface area (a deep tank will not be able to hold significantly more fish than a shallower one).

● The size of the fish.

● Aeration and filtration, which will increase the oxygen content of the water. This will allow up to 40 per cent more fish to be kept in the tank, but can result in a problem if the filtration breaks down

● Room temperature. The water will hold less oxygen when it is warmer, so will support fewer fish. If artificial lighting is used for the tank, it will tend to heat the water to some extent.

As a general rule, allow one inch of body length of fish (excluding the tail) for each 24 square inches (1cm of fish per 60cm) of surface area. This means that a 2ft by 1ft (60cm x 30cm) tank will have a surface area of 288 sq inches (1800 sq cm), which when divided by 24, will support fish with a total body length of about 12 inches (30cm). Either take my word for this, or use a calculator – I did!

Don't forget that fish grow, so you will have to start off with considerably less than the maximum capacity.

DID YOU KNOW?

Fish have no eyelids or iris, so they can't respond rapidly to sudden changes in light intensity. This is why goldfish will usually dash for cover when the lights come on.

Home at Last

Resist the temptation to just pour the new fish into the aquarium when you get home. Open the top of the bag and leave it floating in the tank for about 20 minutes to let the temperature equalise. Gradually mix the water in the tank with the water in the bag, and then release the fish gently.

Even with a large aquarium it is advisable to just get a couple of fairly small specimens first of all to allow the tank to mature.

Once you are sure that all is well, you can consider adding extra fish, but ensure that your fish supplier has quarantined them first to make sure they are free of disease.

Fish should never be caught in the bare hands, as their scales are very easily damaged and this may give a chance for skin disease to get a hold.

Use a clean jam jar to scoop up the fish, or use a special fish-net that you can purchase from any aquarist store. Obviously, fish should only be out of water for the absolute minimum amount of time, as they are not able to breathe air and will quickly die.

Feeding

A Balanced Diet

Although you may be anxious to see your fish eat their first meal in their new tank, wait until they are settled before trying to feed them, and then only feed them very sparingly. A wide range of manufactured foods can be purchased for feeding goldfish, most of them in flake form and containing a wide range of nutrients to provide a balanced diet. Select one made by a major manufacturer and designed specifically for goldfish.

There is no need to feed anything other than this for the whole of your fish's life, although some people do like to give their fish fresh food as a treat. This is not necessarily a good thing, as it can easily introduce disease or pollute the water. If you do want to give your fish the excitement of catching their own food, purchase daphnia (water fleas) from an aquarium centre rather than catching them in a pond, as they should be free from disease. Do not put so much into the tank that uneaten daphnia decompose in the water, so only buy a small quantity and use it fresh.

Over-feeding

The most common problem of all with keeping goldfish is over-feeding, as uneaten food will rapidly pollute the water and kill the fish. It is essential only to feed as much food as the goldfish will consume in five to ten minutes, and this should be done a couple of times a day. A floating feeding ring will help to keep the food in one part of the tank so that the fish can easily find it.

Algae Control

The great bugbear of fishkeeping is algae, the dreaded green gunge that grows in the tank, particularly if there is excessive light shining on to the water. The most common form will grow as a thin layer on the glass, and although it is not harmful, it will detract from the visual appeal of your goldfish.

Various tools are available to scrape the algae off, and the two most popular methods are either using a razor blade in a special holder on the end of a stick, or using a pair of strong magnets, one with felt on one side that sits on the outside of the tank, and the other that is held against the glass on the inside of the tank by the magnet on the outside, but with an abrasive pad on one surface. When the outer magnet is slid around the glass, the inner one is dragged along and cleans off the debris.

Tank cleaning equipment

Changing the water

Regular water changes are very important, and it is far preferable to change 10-20 per cent of the water every couple of weeks than allowing the tank to get really dirty and then changing the whole lot in one go. If a siphon tube is used to drain off the water, the water can be sucked from the bottom of the tank to remove some of the waste matter that has accumulated there as well.

All that is needed is some plastic tubing about half an inch in diameter, and provided the bucket that you use to collect the waste water is below the level of the tank, once you suck some water up into the tube,

A magnetic pad can be used to clean the tank.

it will continue to run into the bucket. If you don't fancy risking getting a mouthful of tank water, you can immerse the tubing in water to fill it, put a finger over each end, put one end in the tank and the other over the bucket, and release your fingers to allow the water to flow.

Remember that just as when you first filled the tank, you should not use water straight from the tap. Allow the water to stand for a few hours, or add a proprietary dechlorinator.

Leaving Your Fish

Leaving an aquarium for a few days when you are away from home is not a problem, particularly if it is a mature tank that will contain a considerable amount of natural organic material to help feed the fish. Lights can easily be operated by a plug-in timeswitch. It is even possible to purchase automatic battery-operated feeders that will release a predetermined amount of food into the tank on a regular basis.

Breeding

DID YOU KNOW?

Goldfish are usually only aggressive during the breeding season.

It is only possible to sex a goldfish when it is in breeding condition. The abdomen of the female will become swollen with eggs; the male may develop some white spots over the gills and on the front fins. Goldfish are likely to come into breeding condition as the days lengthen in the Spring, and in order to successfully rear any young you need to keep just one pair of fish in a fairly large tank, with the male and female separated by a sheet of glass.

Once the female looks ready to lay her eggs, the male can be put back with the female, where he will chase her frenetically, fertilising the eggs as she lays them. The eggs are the size of pinheads and stick to any plants in the aquarium. They then have to be removed into a separate pre-prepared hatchery tank, or separated from the adults, as they would eat them if allowed.

The eggs develop best in a temperature of about 70 degrees Fahrenheit (21°C), and will hatch in about five days. The fry look like tiny hairs attached to the plants at first, and have their own yolk sacs to feed them for the first few days. They then need special fry food as they become free-swimming.

Common Ailments

Signs of Illness

- Reluctance to feed.
- Thin body, or excessive bloating.
- Gasping at the surface.
- Swimming abnormally.
- Lumps or swelling on the skin.
- Sticky faeces attached to the vent.

Many of the agents that cause disease in goldfish are present in the water at all times, and are only able to get a hold and cause disease if the water quality deteriorates so that the fish's resistance to disease drops. Ensure the water quality is good by avoiding pollution with uneaten food and carrying out regular partial water changes.

Overhesting ●————————

If the water in the tank becomes too warm, the oxygen content will drop and fish will show obvious signs of distress such as gasping at the surface of the water. Shade the tank from sunlight with a cloth, and, if possible, use extra aeration bubbled through the water. If the fish are very distressed, you could float a plastic bag full of ice cubes in the water to lower the temperature reasonably quickly.

Common Ailments

Fungus disease ●───────────────

This is a common cause of death in goldfish. The fungus that causes the condition is usually present in the water, but is only able to get a hold when the fish's normal defences are lowered, such as following injury. The affected areas develop fluffy white tufts of fungus and the fish loses condition.

If only one or two fish in a tank are affected, they should be moved to an isolation tank for treatment, and proprietary anti-fungal products can be purchased from an aquarist shop.

Alternatively, affected fish can be placed in an isolation tank containing some tank water with 3 per cent of salt added for about fifteen minutes. Prepare this by weighing out 30g (2oz) of salt and adding it to one litre of tank water.

Do not use table salt that has iodine added as it can be harmful. Try to avoid the problem occurring by ensuring there are no sharp projections within the tank to damage the scales.

White Spot ●━━━━━━━━━━━━━━━━━━━━━━━━━

This is another common and often fatal disease of goldfish.
It is caused by a parasite in the water that results in tiny
white spots all over the skin, fins and also on the gills. They
irritate the fish and often cause them to rub against rocks or
other objects.

A drug called malachite green is used to treat this
condition, and it is readily available from pet shops that
specialise in fish.

The fish should be treated for at least ten days in the tank
in which they normally live to kill off any parasites there.

Fin Rot ●━━━━━━━━━━━━━━━━━━━━━━━━━━━━

This is a bacterial infection of the fins, which will tend to
eat away at them. Proprietary remedies, salt baths, or in
severe cases, antibiotic treatment from a vet, will often clear
the problem, but close attention must be paid to the
underlying water quality. Damaged fin tissue can slowly
grow back once the infection has cleared.

Dropsy

This is a bloating of the body that can progress to the stage where the scales almost stand on end due to the pressure that builds up. It can be due to one of several conditions, such as heart disease or abdominal tumours, but it is a very serious sign of illness, and affected fish are best destroyed as soon as they show signs of distress.

Swim Bladder Disease

The swim bladder is an air-filled sac within the body of the fish that controls their buoyancy. Fish with an inflamed swim bladder lose their sense of balance, and sometimes even swim upside down. The condition is particularly common among the more fancy breeds of goldfish and sometimes rights itself after a few days. Saltwater baths (as previously described) and keeping affected fish in shallow water may help.

Many veterinary surgeries are happy to offer advice on health problems relating to fish, although they will have to actually see a fish in order to supply a prescription drug for treatment. You will also find experienced fishkeepers via your local aquarist society, the address of which you can probably find at the library.